Editor

Eric Migliaccio

Managing Editor

Ina Massler Levin, M.A.

Cover Artist

Brenda DiAntonis

Art Production Manager

Kevin Barnes

Imaging

James Edward Grace

FLUENCY PRACTICE

- Readers' Theater
- Nursery Rhymes
- Poems
- Haiku
- Songs
- Proverbs
- Fables
- Tongue Twisters
- Fairy Tales

Publisher

Mary D. Smith, M.S. Ed.

Author

Melissa Hart, M.F.A.

Teacher Created Resources, Inc.

6421 Industry Way

Westminster, CA 92683

www.teachercreated.com

ISBN: 978-1-4206-8041-6

©2006 Teacher Created Resources, Inc.

Reprinted, 2011

Made in U.S.A.

Table of Contents

Table of Contents (cont.)

Introduction

Fluency is the ability to express oneself easily and gracefully. A fluent reader demonstrates confidence with written material, based on knowledge and practice. *Fluency Practice, Grades 2 and 3* offers beginning readers the opportunity to perfect their oral reading skills in a variety of genres, including:

❖ Nursery Rhymes   ❖ Proverbs

❖ Poetry   ❖ Tongue Twisters

❖ Haiku   ❖ Fairy Tales

❖ Songs   ❖ Readers' Theater

As children practice reading each passage aloud, pay attention to their speed. A fluent reader speaks at a comfortable pace, modulating tone periodically. Encourage children to vary their voice when reading dialog, in particular. This is particularly effective in adding interest for both readers and listeners when approaching reader's theater and short stories.

Note whether children hesitate between words. The practice of each piece in this book will ensure smooth, fluid reading at a consistent pace. Pay attention to the number of words pronounced correctly. The fluent child will read with 90–100% accuracy.

Reading aloud can be intimidating for beginners. The pieces in this book are designed to engage children in the reading process with humor, compelling plots, and exciting new words. Encourage children to read each selection several times as a group, in order to build their familiarity with vocabulary and themes. As each child begins to read aloud individually, use positive reinforcement to reward effort and fluency. After each student finishes an oral reading assignment, congratulate the accomplishment and ask the following questions:

✔ *How do you feel about the way you read the piece?*

✔ *Did you read slowly or quickly?*

✔ *Was your reading choppy or smooth?*

✔ *Did you stumble over particular words?*

✔ *How did you feel about your use of expression? Did you vary your tone?*

✔ *Did you show emotion or feeling?*

✔ *How might you read differently next time?*

Use *Fluency Practice, Grades 2 and 3* to help create enthusiastic and articulate readers.

Before You Read

A nursery rhyme is a traditional song or poem taught to children and handed down from one generation to the next. This poem first appeared in print in 1765. The words "Hey diddle diddle" can be found in Shakespeare's writing!

Hey Diddle Diddle

Hey diddle diddle, the cat and the fiddle,

The cow jumped over the moon.

The little dog laughed to see such fun,

And the dish ran away with the spoon!

Before You Read

This poem is a nursery rhyme in the form of a riddle. It was first published around 1730.

As I Was Going to St. Ives

As I was going to St. Ives,

I met a man with seven wives.

Each wife had seven sacks,

Each sack had seven cats,

Each cat had seven kits.

Kits, cats, sacks, and wives,

How many were going to St. Ives?

Before You Read

In this nursery rhyme, the characters of Jack Sprat and his wife are based on King Charles I and his queen.

Jack Sprat

Jack Sprat could eat no fat,

His wife could eat no lean;

And so betwixt the two of them,

They licked the platter clean.

Jack ate all the lean,

Joan ate all the fat.

The bone they picked it clean,

Then gave it to the cat.

Before You Read
This nursery rhyme refers to Richard, the Duke of York. In 1460, he and his army marched up to his castle during a famous battle.

The Grand Old Duke of York

The grand old Duke of York,

He had ten thousand men.

He marched them up to the top of the hill,

And he marched them down again.

When they were up, they were up,

And when they were down, they were down.

And when they were only halfway up,

They were neither up nor down.

Before You Read

This nursery rhyme was first published in 1841. Haggis, which is mentioned in the second-to-last line of this nursery rhyme, is a traditional Scottish dish. It is made from sheep, and it is somewhat similar to a sausage.

Aiken Drum

There was a man lived in the moon,

And his name was Aiken Drum.

And he played upon a ladle,

and his name was Aiken Drum.

And his hat was made of good cream cheese,

And his name was Aiken Drum.

And his coat was made of good roast beef,

And his name was Aiken Drum.

And his buttons made of penny loaves,

And his name was Aiken Drum.

And his breeches made of haggis bags,

and his name was Aiken Drum.

Before You Read

Edward Lear lived from 1812 to 1888. He was tutored at home and became a famous poet and artist.

The Owl and the Pussy Cat

The Owl and the Pussy Cat went to sea
In a beautiful pea-green boat.
They took some honey, and plenty of money
Wrapped up in a five-pound note.

The Owl looked up to the stars above
And sang to a small guitar,
"O lovely Pussy, O Pussy, my love,
What a beautiful Pussy you are,
You are,
You are!
What a beautiful Pussy you are!"

Pussy said to the Owl, "You elegant fowl!
How charmingly sweet you sing!
O let us be married! too long we have tarried:
But what shall we do for a ring?"

The Owl and the Pussy Cat (cont.)

They sailed away, for a year and a day,
To the land where the Bong-tree grows
And there in a wood a Piggy-wig stood

With a ring at the end of his nose,
His nose,
His nose,
With a ring at the end of his nose.

"Dear Pig, are you willing to sell for one shilling
Your ring?" Said the Piggy, "I will."
So they took it away and were married
next day
By the Turkey who lives on the hill.

They dined on mince and slices of quince,
Which they ate with a runcible spoon;
And hand in hand, on the edge of the sand,
They danced by the light of the moon,
The moon,
The moon,
They danced by the light of the moon.

~Edward Lear

Before You Read

This nursery rhyme was first published in 1805 under the title, "The Comic Adventures of Old Mother Hubbard and Her Dog."

Old Mother Hubbard

Old Mother Hubbard
Went to the cupboard
To fetch her poor dog a bone;
But when she came there
The cupboard was bare,
And so the poor dog had none.

She went to the grocer's
To buy him some fruit;
But when she came back,
He was playing the flute.

She went to the tailor's
To buy him a coat,
But when she came back,
He was riding the goat.

She went to the barber's
To buy him a wig,
But when she came back,
He was dancing a jig.

The dame made a curtsey,
The dog made a bow;
The dame said, "Your servant."
The dog said, "Bow wow!"

~Sarah Catherine Martin

Before You Read

A poem often uses rhythm and rhyme to tell a story. Lewis Carroll was the pen-name of Charles Lutwich Dodgson. This poem appeared in his novel Alice in Wonderland.

Beautiful Soup

Beautiful Soup, so rich and green,
Waiting in a hot tureen!
Who for such dainties would not stoop?
Soup of the evening, beautiful Soup!
Soup of the evening, beautiful Soup!
Beautiful Soup! Who cares for fish,
Game, or any other dish?
Who would not give all else for two
Pennyworth only of Beautiful Soup?

~Lewis Carroll

Before You Read

Laura E. Richards' mother, Julia Ward Howe, was also a poet.

Eletelephony

Once there was an elephant,
Who tried to use the telephant—
No! No! I mean an elephone
Who tried to use the telephone—
(Dear me! I am not certain quite
That even now I've got it right.)

Howe'er it was, he got his trunk
Entangled in the telephunk;
The more he tried to get it free,
The louder buzzed the telephee—
(I fear I'd better drop the song
Of elephop and telephong!)

~Laura E. Richards

Before You Read

*American poet Carl Sandburg traveled across the country as a hobo
before becoming a writer.*

Fog

The fog comes

on little cat feet.

It sits looking

over harbor and city

on silent haunches,

and then moves on.

~Carl Sandburg

Before You Read

Robert Frost loved to write about the people and landscapes of New England.

Good Hours

I had for my winter evening walk—

No one at all with whom to talk,

But I had the cottages in a row

Up to their shining eyes in snow.

And I thought I had the folk within:

I had the sound of a violin;

I had a glimpse through curtain laces

Of youthful forms and youthful faces.

I had such company outward bound.

I went till there were no cottages found.

I turned and repented, but coming back

I saw no window but that was black.

Over the snow my creaking feet

Disturbed the slumbering village street

Like profanation, by your leave,

At ten o'clock of a winter eve.

~Robert Frost

Before You Read
Robert Louis Stevenson was born in Scotland in 1850. He is famous for both his novels and his poetry.

A Good Play

We built a ship upon the stairs

All made of the back-bedroom chairs,

And filled it full of soft pillows

To go a-sailing on the billows.

We took a saw and several nails,

And water in the nursery pails;

And Tom said, "Let us also take

An apple and a slice of cake;"—

Which was enough for Tom and me

To go a-sailing on, till tea.

We sailed along for days and days,

And had the very best of plays;

But Tom fell out and hurt his knee,

So there was no one left but me.

~Robert Louis Stevenson

Before You Read

Sometimes, a poem is passed down from generation to generation but the author's name is lost.

Michael Finnegan

There was an old man named Michael Finnegan
He had whiskers on his chinnegan
They fell out and then grew in again
Poor old Michael Finnegan
Begin again.

There was an old man named Michael Finnegan
He went fishing with a pinnegan
Caught a fish and dropped it in again
Poor old Michael Finnegan
Begin again.

There was an old man named Michael Finnegan
He grew fat and then grew thin again
Then he died and had to begin again
Poor old Michael Finnegan
Begin again.

~Anonymous

18

Before You Read

When the name of the author is unknown, the word "Anonymous" is used in place of a name. "Monday's Child" was a rhyme created to help children learn the days of the week through the use of rhyme.

Monday's Child

Monday's child is fair of face,

Tuesday's child is full of grace,

Wednesday's child is full of woe,

Thursday's child has far to go,

Friday's child is loving and giving,

Saturday's child works hard for a living,

But the child that's born on the Sabbath day

Is bonny, blithe, good, and gay.

~*Anonymous*

Before You Read

This poem refers to a practice used at banquets in the past. Live birds were cooked in a piecrust that, when cut, would allow the birds to fly out.

Sing a Song of Sixpence

Sing a song of sixpence,

A pocket full of rye;

Four and twenty blackbirds

Baked in a pie!

When the pie was opened

The birds began to sing;

Was not that dainty dish

To set before the king?

The king was in his counting-house

Counting all his money;

The queen was in the parlor,

Eating bread and honey.

The maid was in the garden,

Hanging out the clothes;

When down came a blackbird

And snapped off her nose.

~Anonymous

Before You Read

William Blake was an English poet who lived from 1757 to 1827. There are different versions of this poem that have different spellings for the words "watered" and "outstretched." It is thought that the original words were spelled "water'd" and "outstretch'd," or even "waterd" and "outstretchd," but the most common spelling is used below. Think about what he might be saying about friends and enemies in this poem.

A Poison Tree

I was angry with my friend:
I told my wrath, my wrath did end.
I was angry with my foe:
I told it not, my wrath did grow.

And I watered it in fears,
Night and morning with my tears:
And I sunned it with smiles
And with soft deceitful wiles.

And it grew both day and night,
Till it bore an apple bright.
And my foe beheld it shine,
And he knew that it was mine—
And into my garden stole
When the night had veiled the pole;
In the morning, glad, I see
My foe outstretched beneath the tree.

~William Blake

Before You Read

Robert Louis Stevenson was primarily an essayist, but he did write a few books of poems. His most famous is called "A Child's Garden of Verses."

Summer Sun

Great is the sun, and wide he goes
Through empty heaven with repose;
And in the blue and glowing days
More thick than rain he showers his rays.
Though closer still the blinds we pull
To keep the shady parlour cool,
Yet he will find a chink or two
To slip his golden fingers through.
The dusty attic spider-clad
He, through the keyhole, maketh glad;
And through the broken edge of tiles
Into the laddered hay-loft smiles.
Meantime his golden face around
He bares to all the garden ground,
And sheds a warm and glittering look
Among the ivy's inmost nook.
Above the hills, along the blue,
Round the bright air with footing true,
To please the child, to paint the rose,
The gardener of the World, he goes.

~Robert Louis Stevenson

Before You Read

This is thought to be a children's song from the 1880s by George Cooper. It is full of personification, which is when non-human objects or things are given human qualities. An example of this is when the wind speaks to the leaves and tells them to put on their autumn dresses.

An Autumn Greeting

"Come," said the Wind

to the Leaves one day.

"Come over the meadow,

and we will play.

Put on your dresses

of red and gold,

For summer is gone

and the days grow cold."

~Anonymous

Before You Read

Originally trained to be a lighthouse engineer, Robert Louis Stevenson instead wanted to study law and was admitted in 1875. A few years later, he abandoned law for literature.

Winter Time

Late lies the wintry sun a-bed,
A frosty, fiery sleepy-head;
Blinks but an hour or two; and then,
A blood-red orange, sets again.

Before the stars have left the skies,
At morning in the dark I rise;
And shivering in my nakedness,
By the cold candle, bathe and dress.

Close by the jolly fire I sit,
To warm my frozen bones a bit;
Or with a reindeer-sled, explore
The colder countries round the door.

When to go out, my nurse doth wrap
Me in my comforter and cap,
The cold wind burns my face, and blows
Its frosty pepper up my nose.

Black are my steps on silver sod;
Thick blows my frosty breath abroad;
And tree and house, and hill and lake,
Are frosted like a wedding-cake.

~Robert Louis Stevenson

Before You Read

Poet and novelist William Makepeace Thackeray was born in India in 1811. He most liked to do two things when he was a boy: draw and read stories. Here is his poem about the zoo.

At the Zoo

First I saw the white bear, then I saw
the black;
Then I saw the camel with a hump upon
his back;
Then I saw the grey wolf, with mutton in
his maw;
Then I saw the wombat waddle in the straw;
Then I saw the elephant a-waving of
his trunk;
Then I saw the monkeys—mercy, how
unpleasantly they—smelt!

~William Makepeace Thackeray

Before You Read

Kilkenny is a city in Ireland.

Two Cats of Kilkenny

There once were two cats of Kilkenny,
Each thought there was one cat too many,
So they fought and they fit,
And they scratched and they bit,
Till, excepting their nails
And the tips of their tails,
Instead of two cats, there weren't any.

~Anonymous

Before You Read

Christina Rossetti was born in London, in 1830. She was the youngest child in a family of poets and artists.

Caterpillar

Brown and furry
Caterpillar in a hurry,
Take your walk
To the shady leaf, or stalk,
Or what not,
Which may be the chosen spot.
No toad spy you,
Hovering bird of prey pass by you;
Spin and die,
To live again a butterfly.

~Christina Rossetti

Before You Read

Born in Edinburgh, Scotland, in 1850, Robert Louis Stevenson died 44 years later on a small Samoan Island in the Pacific. He once said, "I love the art of words."

The Cow

The friendly cow, all red and white,
I love with all my heart:
She gives me cream with all her might,
To eat with apple tart.

She wanders lowing here and there,
And yet she cannot stray,
All in the pleasant open air,
The pleasant light of day;

And blown by all the winds that pass
And wet with all the showers,
She walks among the meadow grass
And eats the meadow flowers.

~Robert Louis Stevenson

Before You Read

Herbert Asquith was a poet, novelist, and lawyer. Read this poem and think about what type of dog he might have owned.

The Hairy Dog

My dog's so furry I've not seen

His face for years and years:

His eyes are buried out of sight,

I only guess his ears.

When people ask me for his breed,

I do not know or care:

He has the beauty of them all

Hidden beneath his hair.

~Herbert Asquith

Before You Read

Though the original author of this poem is unknown, Bob Dylan rewrote it and put it to music in 1992.

A Frog Went A-Courtin'

A frog went a-courtin', and he did ride

Sword and pistol by his side.

He rode up to Miss Mousie's door,

Where he'd often been before.

He said, "Miss Mouse, are you within?"

"Yes, kind sir, I sit and spin."

He took Miss Mouse upon his knee,

Said "Miss Mouse, will you marry me?"

"Without my Uncle Rat's consent,

I wouldn't marry the President."

Uncle Rat, he laughed and shook his fat sides

To think his niece would be a bride.

Then Uncle Rat rode off to town

To buy his niece a wedding gown.

~Anonymous

Before You Read

Hillaire Belloc was born in 1870 in France. He and his sister were taken to England because of the Franco-Prussian War.

The Elephant

When people call this beast to mind,

They marvel more and more

At such a little tail behind,

So large a trunk before.

~Hillaire Belloc

Before You Read

Haiku is a form of poetry from ancient Japan.

Caterpillar

A caterpillar,

this deep in fall—

still not a butterfly.

~Matsuo Basho

An Old Pond

An old pond;

A frog jumps in—

The sound of water.

~Matsuo Basho

Before You Read

Haiku-master Matsuo Basho lived from 1644 to 1694

The First Cold Shower

The first cold shower;

Even the monkey seems to want

A little coat of straw.

~Matsuo Basho

A Monk Sips Morning Tea

A monk sips morning tea,

it's quiet,

the chrysanthemum's flowering.

~Matsuo Basho

Before You Read

In Japanese, haiku poems follow a strict format of 17 syllables: 5 syllables on the first line, 7 on the second line, and 5 on the third line. In English, which has a variation in length of syllables, this can sometimes be difficult.

O Snail

O snail
Climb Mount Fuji,
But slowly, slowly!

~*Kobayashi Issa*

I Look at the River

I look at the river.
A banana skin
Falls from my hand.

~*Kyoshi Takahama*

Before You Read

Each haiku must contain a kigo, or season word, indicating in which season the haiku is set. The kigo is not always obvious.

How Cool it Is!

How cool it is!
A small crab, in the rain,
Climbs on a pine.

~Shiki Masoaka

Short Summer Night

Short summer night.
A dewdrop
On the back of a hairy caterpillar.

~Buson Yosa

Before You Read

Haiku has been described as being "like a photo that captures the essence of what is happening."

A Giant Firefly

A giant firefly:
that way, this way, that way, this —
and it passes by.

~Kobayashi Issa

I Want to Sleep

I want to sleep
Swat the flies
Softly, please.

~Masaoka Shiki

After Killing a Spider

After killing
a spider, how lonely I feel
in the cold of night!

~Masaoka Shiki

Before You Read

What subject matter do the three haiku poems below have in common?

A lovely thing to see:
through the paper window's hole,
the Galaxy.

~Kobayashi Issa

Harvest moon:
around the pond I wander
and the night is gone.

~Matsuo Basho

In all this cool
is the moon also sleeping?
There, in the pool?

~Ryusui

Before You Read

What subject matter do the three haiku poems below have in common?

Sparrow Singing

Sparrow singing—
its tiny mouth
open.

~*Yosa Buson*

Cold night: the wild duck,
sick, falls from the sky
and sleeps awhile.

~*Matsuo Basho*

That Wren

That wren—

looking here, looking there.

You lose something?

~*Kobayashi Issa*

Before You Read

Many beginning writers of haiku try to put too many different ideas into their poems. Masters of haiku say that a good rule is to have two concrete images, but no more than three.

White Blossoms of the Pear

White blossoms of the pear
and a woman in moonlight
reading a letter.

~Yosa Buson

Blossoms at Night

Blossoms at night,
and the faces of people
moved by music.

~Kobayashi Issa

The Oak Tree

The oak tree:
not interested
in cherry blossoms.

~Matsuo Basho

Before You Read

A song lyric is a piece of writing set to music. The Kookaburra is a bird native to Australia.

Kookaburra

Kookaburra sits in the old gum tree.
Merry, merry king of the bush is he.

Laugh, Kookaburra,
Laugh, Kookaburra,
Gay your life must be.

Kookaburra sits in the old gum tree,
Eating all the gumdrops he can see.

Stop, Kookaburra,
Stop, Kookaburra,
Leave some there for me.

~Anonymous

Before You Read

Use your imagination to picture the woman in this traditional song.

She'll Be Comin' Round the Mountain

She'll be comin' round the mountain
When she comes.
She'll be comin' round the mountain
When she comes.
She'll be comin' round the mountain,
She'll be comin' round the mountain,
She'll be comin' round the mountain
When she comes.

She'll be drivin' six white horses
When she comes.
She'll be drivin' six white horses
When she comes.
She'll be drivin' six white horses,
She'll be drivin' six white horses,
She'll be drivin' six white horses
When she comes.

Oh, we'll all go out to greet her
When she comes.
Oh, we'll all go out to greet her
When she comes.
Oh, we'll all go out to greet her,
Oh, we'll all go out to greet her,
Oh, we'll all go out to greet her
When she comes.

~Anonymous

Before You Read

British military officers first sang Yankee Doodle to make fun of the "Yankees" with whom they served during the French and Indian War. The term "doodle" meant a fool. During the Revolutionary War, United States soldiers adopted the song and made it their own. There are over 190 verses in this traditional song.

Yankee Doodle

Yankee Doodle came to town
A-ridin' on a pony;
He stuck a feather in his hat
And called it macaroni.

Yankee Doodle keep it up,
Yankee Doodle Dandy;
Mind the music and the steps
And with the girls be handy.

Father and I went down to camp
Along with Captain Goodwin;
The men and boys all stood around
As thick as hasty pudding.

Yankee Doodle, keep it up,
Yankee Doodle Dandy;
Mind the music and the steps
And with the girls be handy.

~Anonymous

Before You Read

This song is an American lullaby. It was often sung to help children fall asleep.

Hush, Little Baby

Hush, little baby, don't say a word
Mama's gonna buy you a mockingbird

If that mockingbird don't sing
Mama's gonna buy you a diamond ring

If that diamond ring turns brass,
Mama's gonna buy you a looking glass

If that looking glass gets broke
Mama's gonna buy you a billy goat

If that billy goat don't pull,
Mama's gonna buy you a cart and mule

If that cart and mule turn over
Mama's gonna buy you a dog named Rover

If that dog named Rover won't bark
Mama's gonna buy you a horse and cart

If that Horse and Cart fall down,
Then you'll be the sweetest little baby in town.

~Anonymous

Billy Boy

Oh, where have you been, Billy Boy, Billy Boy?
Oh, where have you been, charming Billy?
"I have been to seek a wife, she's the joy of my life,
She's a young thing and cannot leave her mother."

Can she make a cherry pie, Billy Boy, Billy Boy?
Can she make a cherry pie, charming Billy?
"She can make a cherry pie,
quick as a cat can wink an eye,
She's a young thing and cannot leave her mother."

How old is she, Billy Boy, Billy Boy?
How old is she, charming Billy?
"Three times six and four times seven,
twenty-eight and eleven,
She's a young thing and cannot leave her mother."

~Anonymous

Before You Read

This is a traditional tune, first published in 1844. It was inspired by frontier women, who were notably rugged, high-spirited, and hard working.

Buffalo Gals

As I was walking down the street,
Down the street, down the street,
A pretty gal I chanced to meet
Under the silver moon.

Buffalo gals, won't you come out tonight?
Come out tonight, come out tonight?
Buffalo gals, won't you come out tonight
And dance by the light of the moon?

I asked her if she'd be my wife,
Be my wife, be my wife
Then I'd be happy all my life,
If she'd marry me.

Buffalo gals, won't you come out tonight?
Come out tonight, come out tonight?
Buffalo gals, won't you come out tonight
And dance by the light of the moon?

~Anonymous

I've Been Workin' on the Railroad

I've been workin' on the railroad
All the live long day.
I've been workin' on the railroad,
Just to pass the time away.
Don't you hear the whistle blowing?
Rise up so early in the morn.
Don't you hear the captain shouting
"Dinah, blow your horn"?
Dinah, won't you blow,
Dinah, won't you blow,
Dinah, won't you blow your horn?
Dinah, won't you blow,
Dinah, won't you blow,
Dinah, won't you blow your horn?
Someone's in the kitchen with Dinah.
Someone's in the kitchen, I know.
Someone's in the kitchen with Dinah
Strumming on the old banjo.
Fee, fie, fiddle-e-i-o.
Fee, fie, fiddle-e-i-o.
Fee, fie, fiddle-e-i-o.
Strumming on the old banjo.

~Anonymous

Before You Read

This 18th century song is also a popular dance tune.

Soldier's Joy

Love somebody, yes I do.
Love somebody, and it may be you.

Twice 16's 32.
Sally, won't you have me? Do, gal, do.

Dance all night and fiddle all day—
That's the soldier's joy, they say.

Sun comes up and the moon goes down,
See my little Sally in her morning gown.

Twice 16's 32.
Sally, won't you have me? Do, gal, do.

Dance all night and fiddle all day—
That's the soldier's joy, they say.

If somebody comes and finds me gone,
They better leave my girl alone.

Twice 16's 32.
Sally, won't you have me? Do, gal, do.

Dance all night and fiddle all day—
That's the soldier's joy, they say.

~Anonymous

Before You Read

This is a popular scouting song. It is sung to the tune of "On Top of Old Smokey."

On Top of Spaghetti

On top of spaghetti
All covered with cheese,
I lost my poor meatball
When somebody sneezed.

It rolled off the table
And onto the floor,
And then my poor meatball
Rolled right out the door!

It rolled in a garden
And under a bush.
Now my poor meatball
Was nothing but mush.

The mush was as tasty
As tasty could be.
Early next summer
It grew into a tree.

So if you like spaghetti
All covered with cheese,
Hold on to your meatballs
And don't ever sneeze!

~Anonymous

Before You Read
A short proverb is usually one sentence, and it delivers a moral.

Practice makes perfect.

Slow and steady wins the race.

All's well that ends well.

Honesty is the best policy.

Before You Read

These proverbs all have a message about caution and prudence.

Don't bite the hand that feeds you.

Better be safe than sorry.

No news is good news.

Don't put off until tomorrow what you can do today.

A penny saved is a penny earned.

Before You Read

All of these proverbs are about birds, but each carries a different message.

A bird in the hand is worth two in the bush.

Don't put all your eggs in one basket.

Don't count your chickens before they're hatched.

Birds of a feather flock together.

The early bird catches the worm.

Before You Read

The proverbs below can be used as guidelines for living. Notice, though, that some of the proverbs state the opposite of each other.

Live and learn.

You can't teach an old dog new tricks.

Don't judge a book by its cover.

Experience is the best teacher.

You're never too old to learn.

Before You Read
Many proverbs are about animals. How can you make them connect to your life?

Let sleeping dogs lie.

When the cat's away, the mice will play.

You can lead a horse to water, but you can't make him drink.

A leopard cannot change his spots.

Don't look a gift horse in the mouth.

Before You Read

The following proverbs are a gentle way of scolding someone when they have done or are about to do something wrong.

If you lie down with dogs, you'll wake up with fleas.

Don't throw out the baby with the bathwater.

You can catch more flies with honey than with vinegar.

Bad workers always blame their tools.

Before You Read
All the proverbs below discuss love and its powers.

Love makes the world go 'round.

All you need is love.

Absence makes the heart grow fonder.

Love conquers all.

Marry in haste, repent in leisure.

The Bear and the Two Travelers

Two men were traveling together, when a bear met them on their path. One of them climbed into a tree and hid himself in the branches. The other fell flat on the ground.

The bear came up and felt him with his snout and snuffled in his ear. The man held his breath and pretended to be dead. The bear left him, for it is said that bears will not touch a dead body.

When he was gone, the other traveler jumped down from the tree and said, "What did the bear say to you?"
"He gave me this advice," his friend replied. "Never travel with a friend who leaves you in the face of danger."

~Aesop

Before You Read

Early fables were often written to explain things that couldn't be explained otherwise.

The Hare and the Tortoise

The Hare boasted of his speed in front of the other animals. "I have never been beaten," said he. "I challenge any one here to race with me."

The Tortoise said, "I accept your challenge."

"That is a good joke," said the Hare. "I could dance 'round you all the way."

"Save your boasting until you've beaten me," answered the Tortoise.

They marked a course and started the race. The Hare darted out of sight at once, but soon stopped. To scorn the Tortoise, he lay down to have a nap.

The Tortoise plodded on. When the Hare awoke from his nap, he saw the Tortoise near the finish line. The Hare could not catch him in time.

Then said the Tortoise: "Slow and steady wins the race."

~Aesop

Before You Read

This fable is about a crow that invents an ingenious way of getting water out of a pitcher. Did you know that most inventions were actually mistakes? Post-It Notes stemmed from a failed super glue experiment, and Popsicles came to be when a boy, stirring his cup of fruit-flavored soda, left it out in the cold overnight and came back to find it frozen with the stirring stick standing straight up in it!

The Crow and the Pitcher

A thirsty crow saw a pitcher. Hoping to find water, he flew to it happily. But he saw that it held just a little water. He tried everything he could think of to reach the water, but none of his plans worked.

At last he took as many stones as he could carry. He dropped them one by one with his beak into the pitcher.

Finally, he brought the water within his reach. Then, he took a long, long drink.

Moral: Creative minds find rewards.

~Aesop

Before You Read

In the book, Where the Red Fern Grows, a boy and his grandfather catch a raccoon in the same way the boy was "caught" in this fable. A filbert is a type of nut.

The Boy and the Filberts

A boy put his hand into a pitcher full of filberts. He grasped as many as he could hold. He tried to pull out his hand, but it wouldn't fit through the neck of the pitcher.

Unwilling to drop the filberts but unable to withdraw his hand, he burst into tears.

A friend then said to him, "Drop half the filberts, and you can pull out your hand."

Moral: Do not attempt too much at once.

~Aesop

Before You Read

Aesop was an ancient Greek writer who told dozens of fables.

The Milk-Woman and Her Pail

A farmer's daughter carried her pail of milk from the field to the farmhouse. She began daydreaming. "The money from this milk will buy three hundred eggs. The eggs will produce two hundred and fifty chickens. By the end of the year I shall have money to buy a new gown. I will go to Christmas parties, where all the young men will propose to me—but I will toss my head and refuse them every one."

Then, she tossed her head, and the milk pail fell to the ground. All her dreams vanished.

Before You Read

Aesop's fables remain popular hundreds of years later. This fable was demonstrated in the animated film called A Bug's Life.

The Ant and the Grasshopper

In a field one day, Grasshopper was hopping about, chirping and singing. Ant passed by, carrying an ear of corn to his nest.

"Come chat with me," said Grasshopper, "instead of working so hard."

"I am putting away food for the winter," said Ant. "You should do the same."

"Who cares about winter?" said Grasshopper. "We have plenty of food now." But Ant went on working.

When winter came, Grasshopper had no food. "I'm starving," it said. Then Ant walked by, eating dried corn from its nest.

Now Grasshopper knew that it pays to be prepared.

~Aesop

Before You Read

The term "sour grapes," which means to deny your desire for something because you can't get it, was derived from this fable.

The Fox and the Grapes

One hot summer's day, Fox was walking through an orchard when he came to a bunch of grapes ripe and purple on a vine. "Just the thing to quench my thirst," he said.

Fox took a run and a jump but missed the bunch. He turned around again and cried, "One, Two, Three!" He jumped up but missed the grapes again. Once more, Fox tried to reach the tempting grapes. At last, he gave up and walked away with his nose in the air, saying: "I am sure those grapes are sour."

Moral: It is easy to scorn what you cannot get.

~Aesop

Before You Read

Many of Aesop's fables were about birds. A second moral to this fable can also be summed up by this statement: "Beauty is in the eye of the beholder."

The Peacock and the Crane

A Peacock and a Crane stood by the river, enjoying the sunset. The Peacock spread out its beautiful tail and said vainly, "I am clothed in gold and purple and all the colors of the rainbow, while you are only plain white."

The Crane looked from her own pale feathers to the colorful feathers of the Peacock before her. "This is true," she replied. "But I can fly high up into the sky, while you can only walk along the ground below."

Then, with a hop and a skip, the Crane took off toward the clouds. Circling around, she delivered one last moral to the Peacock:

"Fine feathers don't make fine birds!" she said.

~Aesop

Before You Read

A tongue twister is a phrase that is hard to say quickly because of alliteration or similar sounds.

Big black rubber baby bumpers
burned rubber.

She sells sea shells on the sea shore.

A cricket critic licked a crinkled ticket.

A proper cup of coffee from a
copper coffee pot.

Before You Read

Tongue twisters are often used in speech therapy or given to people who want to work on getting rid of an accent.

Polly Pitcher pitched plump purple plums.

Eight gray geese grew greedy over gravy.

Silly Sally served salty seal soup.

The Big Book Crook took the big cookbook.

Before You Read

The second tongue twister on this page brings up the fact that a woodchuck is an animal that has no ability to "chuck" (toss, throw) wood. How do you think the author came up with the idea for this poem?

A black bug bit a big black bear. But where is the big black bear that the big black bug bit?

How much wood could a wood chuck chuck if a wood chuck could chuck wood?

Before You Read

Fuzzy-Wuzzy was also the name of a character in a ballad by Rudyard Kipling, and Peter Piper was also a superhero who was a normal boy armed with magical pipes.

Fuzzy Wuzzy was a bear. Fuzzy Wuzzy had no hair. Fuzzy Wuzzy wasn't very fuzzy, was he?

Peter Piper picked a peck of pickled peppers. If Peter Piper picked a peck of pickled peppers, where's the peck of pickled peppers Peter Piper picked?

Before You Read

Tongue twisters are often used when someone is learning a language so they can practice repeating one sound at a time.

Six sharp, shifty sharks squashed
a school of shrimp.

Plump pumpkins ponder pitiful perils.

Shirley sheared six soiled sheep
in the shiny sheep shed.

Baby Boy Blue blew big bright bubbles.

Before You Read

Can you "twist" your tongue around these? Say this slowly at first, then increase your speed. What happens to the words the faster you read?

A certain young fellow named Beebee

Wished to marry a lady named Phoebe.

"But," he said. "I must see

What the minister's fee be

Before Phoebe be Phoebe Beebee!"

Before You Read

This tongue twister is also a type of poem called a limerick. All limericks have five lines, two that rhyme each other and another three that rhyme each other. Listen to the cadence of the poem as you read it out loud.

A canner exceedingly canny

One morning remarked to his granny,

"A canner can can

Anything that he can,

But a canner can't can a can, can he?"

Before You Read

It is illegal in most states to own a pet skunk. In the states where it is legal, you must get a permit first.

A skunk sat on a stump.

The skunk thunk the stump stunk,

But the stump thunk the skunk stunk.

Before You Read

It takes 21 pounds of cow's milk to make one pound of butter. There are records of butter's use as early 2000 B.C.

Betty Botter had some butter,
"But," she said, "this butter's bitter.
If I bake this bitter butter,
It would make my batter bitter.
But a bit of better butter,
That would make my batter better."
So she bought a bit of butter —
Better than her bitter butter —
And she baked it in her batter;
And the batter was not bitter.
So 'twas better Betty Botter
Bought a bit of better butter.

Before You Read

A ballad is a song or poem that tells a story. A ballad is sung over centuries, and undergoes changes with each new singer. "The Three Ravens" was first published in 1611.

The Three Ravens

Three ravens sat upon a tree,

Hey down, hey derry day.

Three ravens sat upon a tree,

Hey down.

Three ravens sat upon a tree,

And they were black as black could be.

And sing lay doo and in doo and day.

Before You Read

This ballad was sometimes performed as a play in Ohio during the mid-1800s

Arkansas Traveler

Once upon a time in Arkansas,
An old man sat in his little cabin door
And fiddled at a tune that he liked to hear,
A jolly old tune that he played by ear.

It was raining hard, but the fiddler didn't care—
He sawed away at the popular air.
Though his roof tree leaked like a waterfall
That didn't seem to bother that man at all.

A traveler was riding by that day
And stopped to hear him a-practicing away.
The cabin was afloat, and his feet were wet,
But still the old man didn't seem to fret.

So the stranger said: "Now, the way it seems to me,
You'd better mend your roof," said he.
"Get busy on a day that is fair and bright,
Then pitch the old roof till it's good and tight."

But the old man kept on a-playing at his reel
And tapped the ground with his leathery heel.
"Get along," said he, "for you give me a pain;
My cabin never leaks when it doesn't rain."

Before You Read

American poet Laura E. Richards lived from 1850 to 1943.

Antonio

Antonio, Antonio,
Was tired of living alonio.
He thought he would woo Miss Lissamy Loo
Miss Lissamy Lucy Molonio.

Antonio, Antonio,
Rode off on his polo-polonio.
He found the fair maid in a bowery shade,
A-sitting and knitting alonio.

Antonio, Antonio,
Said, "If you will be my ownio,
I'll love you true, And I'll buy for you,
An icery creamery conio!"

"Oh, nonio, Antonio!...
You're far too bleak and bonio!
And all that I wish, You singular fish,
Is that you will quickly begonio."

Antonio, Antonio,
He uttered a dismal moanio;
Then ran off and hid (Or I'm told that he did)
In the Anticatarctical Zonio.

~Laura E. Richards

Before You Read

This song dates back to the 1700s. Legend says the sight of a mermaid meant a certain shipwreck.

The Mermaid

'Twas Friday morn when we set sail,

And we had not got far from land

When the Captain, he spied a lovely mermaid

With a comb and a glass in her hand.

Then up spoke the Captain of our gallant ship,

And a jolly old Captain was he:

"I have a wife in Salem town,

But tonight a widow she will be."

Then three times 'round went our gallant ship,

And three times 'round went she,

And the third time that she went 'round,

She sank to the bottom of the sea.

~Anonymous

Before You Read

This ballad first appeared in print in 1827. Variations appear in Scotland, Sweden, and the Appalachian Mountains.

The Smart Schoolboy

"Oh, where be you going?"
Said the knight on the road.
"I be going to school,"
Said the boy as he stood.
"Oh, what do you there?"
Said the knight on the road.
"I read from my book"
Said the boy as he stood.
"Oh, what have ye got?"
Said the knight on the road.
"'Tis a bite of bread and cheese."
Said the boy as he stood.
"Oh, pray give me some"
Said the knight on the road.
"Oh no, not a crumb."
Said the boy as he stood.
And he stood and he stood
And 'twas well that he stood,
"Oh no, not a crumb,"
Said the boy as he stood.

~Anonymous

Before You Read

This is Australia's national ballad. Even though it may seem like this ballad is filled with nonsense words, the words are actually real terms, most of which are still used in Australia. The song is about a man who steals a sheep and gets caught by the police.

Waltzing Matilda

Once a jolly swagman camped by a billabong
Under the shade of a coolibah tree,
And he sang as he watched and waited 'til
his billy boiled,
"You'll come a-waltzing Matilda with me."

Down came a jumbuck to dri-ink at that billabong.
Up jumped the swagman and grabbed him with glee,
And he sang as he stuffed that jumbuck in his
tucker-bag,
"You'll come a-waltzing Matilda with me."

Up rode the squatter, mounted on his thoroughbred.
Up rode the troopers, one, two, three.
"Where's that jolly jumbuck you've got in
your tucker-bag?"
"You'll come a-waltzing Matilda with me."

Up jumped the swagman and sprang into
that billabong.
"You'll never take me alive!" said he.

And his ghost may be heard as you pass
by that billabong.
"You'll come a-waltzing Matilda with me."

~Banjo Paterson

Before You Read

"Casey Jones" is based on a Mississippi train wreck in 1900.

Casey Jones

Casey Jones, he loved a locomotive.
Casey Jones, a mighty man was he.
Casey Jones run his final locomotive
With the Cannonball Special on the old I.C.

They pulled out of Memphis nearly two hours late,
Soon they were speeding at a terrible rate.
And the people knew by the whistle's moan.
That the man at the throttle was Casey Jones.

On April 30, 1900, that rainy morn,
Down in Mississippi near the town of Vaughan,
Sped the Cannonball Special only two minutes late
Traveling 70 miles an hour when they saw a freight.

The caboose number 83 was on the main line,
Casey's last words were "Jump, Sim, while you have
the time."
At 3:52 that morning came the fateful end;
Casey took his farewell trip to the promised land.

Casey Jones, he died at the throttle,
With the whistle in his hand.
Casey Jones, he died at the throttle,
But we'll all see Casey in the promised land.

~Wallace Saunders

Before You Read

People sang this ballad at work in the late 1800s.

John Henry

John Henry was a railroad man,
He worked from six 'til five.
"Raise 'em up bullies and let 'em drop down—
I'll beat you to the bottom or die."
John Henry said to his captain:
"You are nothing but a common man.
Before that steam drill shall beat me down,
I'll die with my hammer in my hand."
John Henry said to the Shakers:
"You must listen to my call.
Before that steam drill shall beat me down,
I'll jar these mountains till they fall."
John Henry's captain came to him
With fifty dollars in his hand.
He laid his hand on his shoulder and said:
"This belongs to a steel-driving man."
John Henry was hammering on the right side,
The big steam drill on the left,
Before that steam drill could beat him down,
He hammered his fool self to death.
John Henry was lying on his deathbed,
He turned over on his side,
And these were the last words John Henry said;
"Bring me a cool drink of water before I die."
They carried John Henry to that new burying ground,
His wife all dressed in blue;
She laid her hand on John Henry's cold face,
"John Henry, I've been true to you."

Before You Read

A fairy tale is a story about legendary creatures and deeds.

The Lion and the Mouse

One day a Lion lay asleep in the jungle. A Mouse ran over the Lion's head and down his nose.

The Lion awoke with a roar. Down came his paw over the little Mouse. The great beast was about to swallow the tiny creature. "Pardon me, King, I beg of you," cried the Mouse. "If you will forgive me this time, I will never forget your kindness. If you will spare my life, perhaps I may help you, too."

The Lion began to laugh. "How could a tiny creature like you do anything to help me?" He looked down at the frightened Mouse. "Oh, well. You're not much of a meal, anyway." He took his paw off the poor little Mouse, who quickly scampered away.

Some time after this, some hunters set up rope nets in the jungle. The Lion, who was hunting for food, fell into the trap. He roared and thrashed, trying to free himself, but with every move he made, the ropes bound him tighter.

The unhappy Lion feared he could never escape. His frightened roars echoed through the jungle. Far away, the tiny Mouse heard the Lion's roars. He ran to see if he could help.

When he discovered the Lion caught in the net, Mouse said to him, "Stop, stop! You must not roar. The hunters will come and capture you. I'll get you out of this trap."

With his sharp little teeth, the Mouse chewed the ropes until they broke. When the Lion had stepped out of the net, the Mouse said, "Now, was I not right?"

"Thank you, good Mouse," said the Lion. "You did help me even though I am big and you are so little. I see now that kindness is always worth while."

~Anonymous

Before You Read

The most popular early version of this tale is the one that Hans Christian Andersen wrote in the book Tales Told For Children, *published in 1835. But there were many versions that were told before then. In the earliest versions, the princess is told by a friend that there will be a pea placed under all of her mattresses, and so she is able to pretend to have not slept a wink.*

The Princess and the Pea

Once upon a time, there was a prince who wanted to marry a princess; but she would have to be a real princess. He traveled all over the world to find one, but nowhere could he get what he wanted. There were princesses enough, but it was difficult to find out whether they were real ones. There was always something about them that was not as it should be.

So he came home again and was sad, for he would have liked very much to have a real princess.

One evening a terrible storm came on; there was thunder and lightning, and the rain poured down in torrents. Suddenly a knocking was heard at the city gate, and the old king went to open it.

It was a princess standing out there in front of the gate. But, good gracious! what a sight the rain and the wind had made her look. The water ran down from her hair and clothes; it ran down into the toes of her shoes and out again at the heels. And yet she said that she was a real princess.

82

The Princess and the Pea *(cont.)*

Well, we'll soon find that out, thought the old queen. But she said nothing, went into the bed-room, took all the bedding off the bedstead, and laid a pea on the bottom; then she took twenty mattresses and laid them on the pea, and then twenty eider-down beds on top of the mattresses.

On this the princess had to lie all night. In the morning she was asked how she had slept.

"Oh, very badly!" said she. "I have scarcely closed my eyes all night. Heaven only knows what was in the bed, but I was lying on something hard, so that I am black and blue all over my body. It's horrible!"

Now they knew that she was a real princess because she had felt the pea right through the twenty mattresses and the twenty eider-down beds.

Nobody but a real princess could be as sensitive as that. So the prince took her for his wife, for now he knew that he had a real princess; and the pea was put in the museum, where it may still be seen, if no one has stolen it.

~Hans Christian Andersen

Before You Read

"The Little Red Hen" likely began as a Russian folk tale and was handed down through the ages.

The Little Red Hen

One day as the Little Red Hen was scratching in a field, she found a grain of wheat.

"This wheat should be planted," she said. "Who will plant this grain of wheat?"

"Not I," said the Duck.

"Not I," said the Cat.

"Not I," said the Dog.

"Then I will," said the Little Red Hen. And she did.

Soon the wheat grew to be tall and yellow.

"The wheat is ripe," said the Little Red Hen. "Who will cut the wheat?"

"Not I," said the Duck.

"Not I," said the Cat.

"Not I," said the Dog.

"Then I will," said the Little Red Hen. And she did.

When the wheat was cut, the Little Red Hen said, "Who will thresh this wheat?"

"Not I," said the Duck.

"Not I," said the Cat.

"Not I," said the Dog.

"Then I will," said the Little Red Hen. And she did.

The Little Red Hen *(cont.)*

When the wheat was all threshed, the Little Red Hen said, "Who'll take this wheat to the mill?"
"Not I," said the Duck.
"Not I," said the Cat.
"Not I," said the Dog.
"Then I will," said the Little Red Hen. And she did.

She took the wheat to the mill and had it ground into flour. Then she said,
"Who will make this flour into bread?"
"Not I," said the, Duck.
"Not I," said the Cat.
"Not I," said the Dog.
"Then I will," said the Little Red Hen. And she did.

She made and baked the bread. Then she said, "Who will eat this bread?"
"Oh! I will," said the Duck.
"And I will," said the Cat.
"And I will," said the Dog.
"No, no!" said the Little Red Hen. "I will do that."
And she did.

Before You Read

In the Brothers Grimm version of "Sleeping Beauty," her name is Brier Rose.

Sleeping Beauty

Once upon a time, there lived a King and Queen. When their baby daughter was born, they threw a big party. They invited their family, their friends, and all the fairies in the land.

There were thirteen fairies altogether, but the king but queen only invited twelve. They forgot about the 13th. That was something they should not have done.

The fairies gathered around the baby's cradle. Each made a magic wish. "The princess shall be beautiful," said the first.

"And happy," said the second.

"And kind," said the third. And so they went on.

Just as the twelfth fairy was about to make her wish, in came the thirteenth. She was angry because she had not been invited. "Here is my wish," she said. "When the princess is sixteen, she will prick her finger on a spindle and die."

Then the twelfth fairy made her wish. "The princess will prick her finger, but she will not die. She will only sleep for a hundred years."

Sleeping Beauty *(cont.)*

The king and queen ordered every spinning wheel and spindle in the land to be burnt. Years passed, and the princess grew up. On her sixteenth birthday, the princess explored the castle. She came to a room at the top of a tower. There was an old woman.

"I am spinning," said the old woman, who was really the thirteenth fairy. "Would you like to try?"

The princess sat down by the spinning wheel. As soon as she touched the spindle, the point pricked her finger and she fell asleep. The king and queen, the servants, the cats and the dogs all fell asleep, too!

Wild roses grew until the castle was hidden. One hundred years passed. One day, a prince rode up and saw the tower rising up above the roses. He jumped off his horse and entered the castle. Everyone was asleep.

He came to the room at the top of a tower and saw the sleeping princess. She was so beautiful that he bent down and kissed her. Then the spell was broken. The princess opened her eyes.

At the same moment, everyone in the castle awoke! The king yawned, the queen blinked, the cats stretched, and the dogs wagged their tails. The princess married the prince, who had woken her from her long, long sleep.

Before You Read

This tale has been around for centuries. In the earliest recorded versions the intruder was either a fox or an old woman. Eventually, in a version published in 1849, the intruder became a little girl named "Silver Hair." Later, she became "Goldilocks."

Goldilocks and the Three Bears

Once upon a time, there was a little girl named Goldilocks. She went for a walk in the forest and came upon a house. She knocked and knocked, but no one answered. She walked right in!

There were three bowls of porridge on the table. Goldilocks was hungry. She tasted the porridge from the first bowl.

"This porridge is too hot!" she cried.

She tasted the porridge from the second bowl.

"This porridge is too cold," she said

She tasted the last bowl of porridge.

"This porridge is just right," she said and ate it all up.

She felt tired, so she walked into the bedroom. She lay down in the first bed. "This bed is too hard!" she cried.

She lay in the second bed. "This bed is too soft," she said.

Goldilocks and the Three Bears *(cont.)*

She lay down in the third bed. "This is just right." Goldilocks fell asleep. Then, the three bears came home.

"Someone's been eating my porridge," growled Papa Bear.

"Someone's been eating my porridge, too," said Mama Bear.

"Someone's been eating my porridge, and they ate it all up!" cried Baby Bear.

They walked into the bedroom. "Someone's been sleeping in my bed," growled Papa Bear.

"Someone's been sleeping in my bed, too," said Mama Bear.

"Someone's been sleeping in my bed—and she's still there!" cried Baby Bear.

Goldilocks woke up and saw the three bears. She screamed. Then she jumped up and ran out of the room.

Goldilocks ran down the stairs, opened the door, and ran off into the forest. And she never returned to the home of the three bears.

Before You Read

Readers' Theater refers to a short script that can be read out loud.
Choose one person to read each character.

The Sock Thief

Characters

- Narrator
- Stripe—a cat
- Sam—a little boy
- Mr. Miller—a neighbor
- Mom—a mother

Narrator: We are in a backyard in a quiet neighborhood. Mom is bringing laundry in from the line. Sam is riding his bike.

Mom: Sam, did you take my sock?

Sam: No, Mom.

Mom: But I hung a pair of red socks two hours ago. Now one is missing.

Sam: I'm sorry. I haven't seen it anywhere.

Mom: Oh, well. Please come in and help me fold this laundry.

Narrator: Sam and Mom go inside to fold clothes. Stripe trots through the backyard with a red sock in his teeth.

Stripe: Ha ha! Look what I've got!

Narrator: That afternoon, Sam has soccer practice. He goes outside to get his cleats.

Sam: Mom, did you take my sock?

Mom: No, Sam.

Sam: But I had a pair of white sports socks stuffed in my cleats. Now one is missing.

Mom: I'm sorry. I haven't seen it anywhere.

Sam: Oh, well. I'll have to wear my blue socks.

The Sock Thief (cont.)

Narrator: Sam goes inside to get his blue socks. Stripe trots through the backyard with a white sock in his teeth.

Stripe: Ha ha! I found another one!

Narrator: Mom and Sam walk down the block toward the park. They see their neighbor, Mr. Miller, pulling weeds in his yard.

Mom: Good afternoon, Mr. Miller.

Sam: Hi, Mr. Miller.

Mr. Miller: Hello, neighbors. How are you?

Mom: Fine, but someone keeps stealing our socks.

Mr. Miller: Is that so? Well, take a look at this!

Narrator: Mr. Miller walks over to his rosebush and bends down. When he stands up, he has two socks in his hand—one red and one white.

Mr. Miller: I just found these buried under my rose bush. Do you recognize them?

Mom: The red one belongs to me.

Sam: The white one belongs to me.

Mr. Miller: That's funny. I've got all my socks, but I'm missing my cat, Stripe. Have you seen him?

Mom and Sam together: No, we haven't seen your cat.

Narrator: From up in an oak tree, Stripe begins to laugh.

Stripe: Ha ha! The sock thief strikes again!

Before You Read

In this readers' theater story, a girl is trying to earn enough money to buy a horse. She does many different jobs and saves all her money. Find out if she saved enough to buy her horse.

Annie's Horse

Characters

- Narrator
- Carlos and Sara—two school friends
- Annie—a little girl
- Ms. Lee and Mr. Sanchez—two neighbors
- Dad—her father

Narrator: Carlos wanted a videogame. Sara wanted her own telephone. But Annie wanted a horse.

Dad: Annie, horses are very expensive. We can't afford one right now.

Annie: Then I will work to buy one myself.

Narrator: Annie built a lemonade stand. She set it up on the corner and made lemonade.

Ms. Lee: I would like to buy a glass. Here is twenty-five cents.

Annie: Thank you, Ms. Lee.

Narrator: Annie dropped a quarter into her piggy bank.

Carlos: Annie, come play videogames with me!

Annie: I'm sorry, I can't today, Carlos. I'm earning money to buy a horse.

Carlos: Too bad.

Narrator: Annie sold eleven more glasses of lemonade that day.

Annie: Dad, I have three dollars! Can we buy a horse?

Dad: Horses cost much more than three dollars.

Narrator: The next weekend, Annie put up a sign that read "Car Wash—50 Cents."

Annie's Horse *(cont.)*

Mr. Sanchez: My old car needs a bath.

Annie: I'd be glad to wash it.

Narrator: Annie washed her neighbor's car, and he handed her two quarters.

Mr. Sanchez: Thanks, Annie! My car looks new again!

Narrator: Then Sara called Annie on her new telephone.

Sara: Annie, come over and we can call all our friends.

Annie: I'm sorry, I can't today, Sara. I'm earning money to buy a horse.

Sara: Too bad.

Narrator: Annie washed seven more cars that day.

Annie: Dad, I earned four more dollars. That makes seven. Can we buy a horse?

Dad: Oh, Annie. Horses are expensive—much more than seven dollars.

Narrator: For the next six months, Annie did odd jobs. She sold hot chocolate. She washed the neighbors' windows. She walked dogs and babysat Ms. Lee's two-year old. She even cashed in bottles and cans at the recycling center. Finally, she went back to her father.

Annie: Dad, I've saved one hundred dollars. Can we please buy a horse now?

Dad: One hundred dollars? That's a lot of money, but it's not enough to buy a horse. Still, . . .

Narrator: The next day, Carlos knocked on the door with his videogame. Sara called on her telephone. Ms. Lee came over to ask if Annie could babysit, and Mr. Sanchez asked if she would wash his car again. To all of them, Annie said the same thing.

Annie: I'm sorry, I can't today. My father is taking me to buy a horse!

Before You Read

This is a story about a being in a new school and not knowing anyone.
Most everyone has felt this way at one time or another.

The New Boy

Characters

- Narrator
- Mr. Norton—a teacher
- Jack, Marisol, and Lin—children in Mr. Norton's class
- Samuel—a new boy in school

Narrator: Samuel's family was new to town. He walked into Mr. Norton's class one morning in the middle of February.

Mr. Norton: You must be Samuel. Welcome to our class.

Samuel: Thank you.

Jack: Look at those thick glasses.

Marisol: His shoes are weird. No one wears those around here.

Lin: I was the new kid last year. It's hard.

Mr. Norton: Samuel, you can sit at the empty desk in the back of the room. Class, let's read aloud until recess.

Narrator: The bell sounded for recess at 10:30. All the children lined up at the door and ran outside to the playground. Samuel stood by himself under a tree.

Jack: He's short. I'll bet he's no good at basketball.

Marisol: He talks funny. I'll bet he's from outer space.

Lin: Don't make fun of him. That's mean. Jack, you should ask him if he wants to play basketball.

Jack: No way. He's too weird. I've got my own friends.

Lin: Marisol, let's ask him if he wants to play on the monkey bars.

Marisol: No way. I've got my own friends, too. Why don't you go ask him to play?

Lin: I'm too shy.

The New Boy (cont.)

Narrator: Recess was almost over. Samuel stood under a tree, watching Jack play basketball with his friends. Lin stood at the edge of the field, watching Samuel. Finally, Lin took a deep breath and walked over to him.

Lin: Hi, Samuel. I'm Lin.

Samuel: Hello.

Lin: I remember what it was like to be the new kid. Last year, I came here from China.

Samuel: I had to leave my friends when my parents decided to move. It's hard to come to a new school.

Lin: Where did you used to live? You have an accent.

Samuel: In Texas. That's funny. To me, you all talk with an accent.

Lin: We do?

Narrator: Lin and Samuel laugh. Just then, Marisol and Jack run up.

Jack: What's so funny?

Marisol: Why are you laughing?

Lin: Samuel says we talk with an accent, too.

Jack and Marisol: Really?

Mr. Norton: Time for class, children.

Narrator: The children line up and walk inside. As they take their seats, Marisol whispers to Samuel.

Marisol: Nice shoes.

Samuel: Thanks. All the kids wore them at my old school. They're great for playing basketball.

Jack: You play basketball?

Samuel: Of course.

Lin: Samuel and I challenge you and Marisol to a game after lunch.

Jack: You're on!

Before You Read

"Meet Paul Bunyan" is an example of a tall tale. The authors of tall tales are usually unknown, because the tales have been told and retold for hundreds of years.

Meet Paul Bunyan

Characters

- Narrator
- Paul Bunyan
- Babe, the Blue Ox

Narrator:	In a time too long ago for even history books, America was one large forest. Thick forests grew across the country, from sea to shining sea. Paul Bunyan was the greatest lumberjack there ever was. He was a mighty giant of a man.
Paul Bunyan:	My name is Paul Bunyan. The greatest lumberjack there ever was! I am a mighty giant of a man.
Narrator:	Paul was so big that it took five giant storks to carry that huge bundle of joy to his parents.
Paul Bunyan:	I am so big, I ate forty barrels of baby cereal as a child.
Narrator:	Paul was so big that he used treetops to comb out his wiry black beard.
Paul Bunyan:	I am so big, on cold days my breath makes steam clouds that block out the sun.
Narrator:	Everywhere Paul went in the wild woods Babe, his blue ox, went.
Paul Bunyan:	Yessiree! This is my trusted friend, Babe.
Babe:	That's me! I am Babe, the blue ox. I am the greatest, bluest beast there ever was.
Narrator:	Babe measured 42 ax handles high. (An ax-handle is about a foot and a half long.) When Babe bellowed, it shook the trees down to their roots.
Babe:	Some folks think they hear thunder. But, no! It's just my bellowing.
Paul Bunyan:	Babe is so strong that he can pull anything that has two ends.
Narrator:	Paul once used Babe to straighten out 30 miles of crooked town road!
Paul Bunyan:	I said, "Babe, you are the greatest, bluest beast ever was. Now you take the end of this crooked road and pull. Pull, Babe, pull! Pull, Babe, pull!"
Babe:	I am so strong, I can pull anything that had two ends. I pulled and pulled.
Narrator:	When Babe had pulled all the twists and curves straight, there were an extra 12 miles of road left over.
Babe:	Paul rolled it all up and gave it back to the town to use elsewhere.
Narrator:	That proves it: Paul Bunyan is a mighty, giant of a man
Paul:	And Babe is the greatest, bluest beast ever was!